Dakota Skies

Books by Joyce Suter Whitcomb

Dakota Skies
Sing Me a Song
Magic Moments
*Prairie Poet: This Land Called South Dakota
and Other Poems*

Dakota Skies

Poems by
Joyce Suter Whitcomb

Illustrated by John E. Suter, Jr.

Exposition Press of Florida   *Pompano Beach, Florida*

First Edition

© 1985 by Joyce Suter Whitcomb

ISBN 0-682-40242-7

Printed in the United States of America

Contents

Preface   vii

Dakota Skies   1
The Larks   3
This Day Is Mine!   4
The Man Who Carved Mount Rushmore   5
Paha Sapa   7
Tribute to a Faithful Bird Dog   9
I'm Going Home to the Black Hills   12
The Wind in the Pines   13
Chapel in the Pines   15
The Storm   16
The Pear Tree   17
Happiness   18
The Folks in My Hometown   21
Hometown, USA   22
The Circle   23
An Old-Fashioned Garden   24
Autumn in the Black Hills   27
Levi Craig Whitcomb   29
The Land That Time Forgot   31
The Sound of Children   33
Summer Is Coming!   34
The Wedding   35
Autumn Romance   37
The Dreamer   38
I've Never Seen the Wind   41
Victory   42
God Is Awake!   42
Going Back Home to the Farm   43
Twilight on the Prairie   45
What Have We Done with Christmas?   46
A Time for Christmas   49
Of Butterflies and Battlefields   51
The Good Shepherd   52
Lord Jesus, Come   53

God's Love 55
The Good Book Says 56
Saints, Be Joyful 57
Hallelujah, Advent Day! 58
Misery 59
Anticipating England 60
The Randolph Hotel 61
My Flower Bed 63
The Quarrel 64
I Thank Thee, Lord 65
The Telephone's Secrets 67
Waiting for Spring 69
The Journey 70
My Choice 71
The Legacy 72

Illustrations

Dakota Skies viii
The Larks 2
Paha Sapa 6
Tribute to a Faithful Bird Dog 8
Chapel in the Pines 14
The Folks in My Hometown 20
Autumn in the Black Hills 26
Levi Craig Whitcomb 28
The Land That Time Forgot 30
Autumn Romance 36
I've Never Seen the Wind 40
Twilight on the Prairie 44
Of Butterflies and Battlefields 50
God's Love 54
Misery 59
My Flower Bed 62
The Telephone's Secrets 66
Waiting for Spring 68

Preface

This book is very special to me because it is the fulfillment of a dream I have had for a long time—to have some of my poems illustrated by my brother, John. He was so much a part of my childhood, and we shared many wonderful times. We grew up in South Dakota at Wind Cave, Mount Rushmore, and the Badlands, where our father was a ranger for the National Park Service. It was a marvelous experience to live so close to nature, surrounded by the beautiful Black Hills—a childhood few are fortunate enough to have. I have tried to capture some of the beauty and magic of that childhood in my poems. I owe a tremendous debt of gratitude to John for sharing his talent with me. For both of us, this truly was a labor of love. With special thanks to our Mother, for her support and encouragement; for painstakingly salvaging our childhood literary efforts and our drawings from obscure wastebaskets; and for always believing that she would one day see them in print.

J Suter

Dakota Skies

Perhaps it only seems that way—
The sky, so black, like velvet,
The stars so close, I can almost touch them,
The air, so soft the slightest breeze caresses
Like a tender kiss.

And, oh, the smell of the pine trees!
Their fragrant needles crackling beneath my feet,
Breaking the stillness of the night;
Somewhere there's a plaintive sound—
A solitary owl.

The night so perfect,
Like no other,
Anywhere.
Only in the Black Hills,
Just the way I remembered,
Long ago, in South Dakota,
The way a night was meant to be.
Perhaps it only seems that way.

The Larks

I heard the larks a singing,
When the storm had just passed by;
They filled the air with music,
'Ere the clouds had left the sky.

They didn't wait for sunshine
To send its warming rays;
They saw the lovely rainbow
And warbled songs of praise.

If the tiny little songbirds
Put their trust in God above,
How much more we ought to trust Him
To surround us with His love.

If the storms of life assail us,
And there's driving wind and rain,
When we hear the larks a singing,
We know the sun will shine again.

This Day Is Mine!

Each new day is a priceless gift,
Wrapped in the bright hues of dawn
And tied with ribbons of sunlight,
Twenty-four beautiful hours, all mine.
Yesterday's happiness, yesterday's sorrows,
They are gone from me, and I can never have them back.

But, I have today, and I am filled with anticipation.
What shall I do? How can I use this gift?
I must not be selfish, for gifts are meant to be shared.
And yet, I would keep a few moments just for myself;
I must renew my spirit. I must commune with God.
Then I will be ready.

As this day unfolds, I am at once the master and the slave;
These hours are my wealth and I must spend wisely.
I cannot draw from the past or borrow from the future;
Only this day is mine, each moment precious.
I will look for flowers and play with children.
I will listen to the song of the lark and feel the wind in my
    hair.

And, as the hours pass like sand through a glass,
I will savor the glowing sunset,
And then, to sleep.
And if, perchance, I do not wake,
It will not matter.
I have had today!
And that is all I need.

The Man Who Carved Mount Rushmore

(Gutzon Borglum)

A man once came to a mountain of stone,
And there was a dream in his mind,
That out of that granite, rough and gray,
Was a gift he would give to mankind.

Now the stuff of which this man was made
Was as stubborn and strong as the stone;
He would conquer that mountain, yes, he would,
For the dream in his heart was his own!

The mountain was high, and the stone was hard,
But the dreamer was stronger still;
So he set to work on the great rock wall,
And the mountain bent to his will.

The doubters beheld the awesome task,
And scoffing, they turned away,
"The mountain is big; he's only a man.
It cannot be done," they would say.

But there where the sun lit the mountain at dawn,
A face slowly came to appear,
And the word went out to the waiting throng,
And the scoffers returned to cheer.

High up on this pile of stones,
Where the tall pines reach the sky,
He carved a shrine for all to see,
For the dream of this man would not die!

The wind and the rain of a thousand years
Will never this shrine erase,
And the children of children yet unborn
Will reverently gaze on each face.

Now when a man's dreams are strong enough,
They become the man's destiny,
And a mountain of stone became a shrine
That will stand 'til eternity.

Paha Sapa

(Black Hills)

Paha Sapa—sacred mountains,
Homeland of the noble Sioux,
Where the towering ponderosa
Pierce the skies forever blue.

Paha Sapa—land of promise
For the white man seeking gold;
To a mine they called "the Homestake"
Came prospectors brash and bold.

Paha Sapa—lovely Black Hills,
Where a dreamer dreamed alone;
He would carve a granite mountain,
Carve a shrine out of the stone.

Paha Sapa—land of sunshine,
Haven for the nimble deer,
Where the mighty bison graze,
By flowing streams so cold and clear.

Paha Sapa—hills of beauty,
Blessed land I used to roam,
Seems to call my restless spirit,
"Come, oh, wanderer, come back home!"

J. Suter

Tribute to a Faithful Bird Dog

(To Lord)

Sleep on, old pal, and take your rest;
You've earned it.
Dear faithful companion of the hunt,
How I am going to miss you!
When the air turns crisp, and the smell of fall is just around
    the corner,
I will be remembering.
The leaves will turn their brightest colors;
The fields of grain will go to harvest;
Hunters will don their suits and oil their guns,
But you will not be there.
You will be sleeping in that special place
At the back of the yard, where the shadows of the big
    oaks
Fall long at eventide,
Where the early morning rays of sunshine
Bring the warmth that you loved so much.
It is a quiet spot.
Nearby are other loved pets gone to rest:
Your mother, Duchess; your sister, Lady; and dear old
    Duke.
But you, Lord, were my special dog.
We shared so many good times, you trotting by my side,
Ready to spring into a point, so eager to please.

Oh, it was grand!
And how you trusted our good friend Charlie, and his
    airplane,
Which took us to such exciting places.
You were never afraid to fly;
You just climbed right in and settled down,
Quivering with anticipation for the hunt that lay ahead.

There were quiet moments that we spent together,
Resting under a tree, you at my feet,

Looking at me with those great brown eyes.
I grieved for you as your sight began to fail,
Those eyes dimmed by cataracts and age.
I remember how bright they were when you were a pup.
You had ten brothers and sisters,
What a litter!
And you caught my fancy with your clumsy little legs,
Always wading into your food with all four paws.
I could tell you were special even then.
Of all those puppies, you were my choice,
And you never proved me wrong,
Not once!
You loved to hunt as much as I did,
But when the season ended, you always knew,
And the rabbits that nested nearby
Never feared that you would molest them.
You seemed to realize that they belonged to us, too.
You shared your food with the birds,
And slept while the squirrels scampered about.
When the mother quail marched her brood proudly across
    the lawn,
You only yawned and went back to dreaming.
The squirrels played games,
Running up and down the trees by your pen;
They knew they had nothing to fear.
You never chased cars or barked at strangers.
You only lived to hunt, to please me.
With your magnificent chest and powerful limbs,
You could go for hours when you were young
And healthy.

Sniffing out the quail, or grouse, or pheasant,
Standing at point and rushing to retrieve,
You could do it all!
We worked together as one mind.
Too soon the signs of age began their toll;
Your great body ravaged by disease.
We did all we could to save you from the pain.

Finally, in mercy, we had you put to sleep.
It was so hard to do, old friend.
And now you rest;
Beneath that mound lies your spent body,
But your great spirit lives on.
And every time I feel fall in the air,
And see the leaves turn brown and drift slowly earthward,
I will be remembering other falls,
When off we'd go together,
Out in the field for our big adventure,
Just the two of us,
Like eager children, we'd romp along.
And at the crack of the gun, you'd be off,
Bringing the quarry to lay at my feet;
And at day's end, we'd sit together,
Satisfied that we had fulfilled that most primitive of urges,
The need to fill the larder.
We were the faithful providers for our family.
It was a joyous time.
Thank you, faithful dog.
Sleep now, you've earned your rest.

There will be other dogs,
Even now, young Princess is in her pen,
Eager and willing, awaiting my command.
There will be more hunts.
But always I will be remembering,
You were my dog, and I loved you.

I'm Going Home to the Black Hills

I'm going home to the Black Hills,
Back to the land of my birth,
Where the air is pure, and the people there
Are the grandest folks on earth!

I'm going home to my mountains,
Where the pines grow tall and green,
Where the water is cold and sparkling,
And it's restful and serene.

I'm going home to the Black Hills,
Where the freshest breezes blow.
I'll see those friends who are dear to me,
And we'll talk of the long ago.

I'm going home to my mountains,
Where the wind makes the treetops sway.
It's there I feel closer to heaven,
And I know God hears when I pray.

When I'm tired of the busy life that I lead,
I know how to lose all my care;
It's time to go home to the Black Hills,
And my soul will find peace when I'm there.

The Wind in the Pines

The sweetest sound I've ever heard
Is the sound of the wind in the pines.
There comes a stirring in my breast,
As memory 'round my heart entwines.

That lovely, lonely, sighing sound,
Like an anthem from above,
As all the trees become God's choir,
To sing of His great love.

And as the breezes softly blow,
My cares just slip away;
My restless soul at last finds peace,
Lulled by the pines' gentle sway.

J. Suter

Chapel in the Pines

There's a place that I call my cathedral,
A secret place I have found,
Deep in the dark green forest,
Far from the city's harsh sound.

The sky above is the ceiling,
The altar is granite stone,
Beauty is there all around me,
And I am with God, alone.

The walls of my forest cathedral
Are the trees that reach to the sky.
I can hear a heavenly chorus,
When the winds in the pines pass by.

The creatures of field and of forest
Come there to worship with me,
To praise our Lord and Creator,
And sing of His majesty.

The birds join in the singing,
An anthem of joy from above;
The babbling brook is my sermon,
While God's presence enfolds me with love.

I go to my forest cathedral
To lose all my worry and care,
And somehow heaven seems nearer,
As I talk to the Savior in prayer.

How lovely is my cathedral,
How precious the hours there I spend,
How great is the love that He shows me,
My Maker, Redeemer, and Friend!

The Storm

I like to snuggle down in bed,
On a dark and gloomy night,
When thunder roars about my head,
And lightning flashes bright.

My bed is like a haven,
Where I am safe and warm;
Within the tight cocoon I make,
I listen to the storm.

Sometimes I like to think
That, once more, I'm a child,
Living on the mountaintop,
Where gales were fierce and wild.

I remember how the mighty wind
Would bend the trees down low,
As lightning bolts across the sky
Lit my room with an eerie glow.

The storms would never frighten me,
Although my heart would pound,
As I listened to the driving rain,
Come pelting to the ground.

All too soon the storm would end;
The sky would turn clear and bright;
My eyes would close in blissful sleep,
Lulled by the storm in the night.

The Pear Tree

Every year, in the early spring,
    My pear tree bursts into bloom,
The first of all of my trees.
And its fragrant, white blossoms,
    Like drifting snow,
Are borne to earth on the balmy breeze.

Then where each blossom fell,
    With delicate grace,
The tiny new pears soon appear,
Each perfectly formed, and
    With succulent promise
For a sun-ripened feast, in the fall
    Of the year!

As spring turns to summer,
    With long, lazy days,
The pears grow fat and round,
And the fruit ladened branches
    Bend way down low,
So low, nearly touching the ground.

And the beady-eyed squirrels,
    And cocky blue jays,
Stay busy from dawn until night;
Like eager gourmets, they choose
    And sample the pears,
Chattering with glee, and delight!

Finally, it's fall,
    And there's frost in the air.
The leaves turn to scarlet and gold,
A last fling of drama,
    Before going to sleep,
While the north winds of winter
    Blow cold!

Happiness

Happiness is home and hearth,
And loved ones gathered 'round;
It's brown beans bubbling in the pot,
And a bluebird's happy sound.

Happiness is clean washed clothes
That smell of freshest air;
It's reaching for your love at night,
And finding he is there.

Happiness is music,
With all the family singing;
It's a pine log crackling on the fire,
And snow the wind is bringing.

Happiness is morning,
And the sun's first golden ray;
It's a meadow filled with clover,
And the smell of new mown hay.

Happiness is the feeling
That you've done your very best;
It's believing that when love is strong,
It can weather any test.

Happiness is strawberries,
Growing wild on the hill;
It's lovely red geraniums
That line the windowsill.

Happiness is having friends
Who you know are always there,
And when you really need them,
They show how much they care.

Happiness is a silver moon
On a crisp, cold winter night;
It's a warm bed to snuggle down in,
And someone to hold you tight.

Happiness is roses red,
And grass that's wet with dew;
It's the sound of children laughing,
And a summer sky so blue.

Happiness is all these things,
And, oh, so many more,
For every blessing we receive
Is but a drop in heaven's store.

The Folks in My Hometown

(Hot Springs, South Dakota)

I've traveled far, I've traveled wide,
O'er hill and dale, upland and down,
And the greatest folks in all the world
Are the folks in my hometown!

Now, I've made friends where ere I've gone,
From the east coast to the west,
But this I've found—and it's from the heart—
The old friends are the best!

They know my faults and weaknesses,
And they love me just the same,
And every time they greet me,
They call me by my name.

They laugh with me in happy times;
They weep when I am sad.
I know that I can count on them
In good times and in bad.

They're always glad to see me;
They rejoice in my success,
And when I've failed at something,
They've never loved me less.

I'll miss those dear sweet gentle folks,
As o'er the world I roam,
But they'll all be there at journey's end,
To welcome me back home.

Hometown, USA

There's a haze on the meadow,
And bees in the clover;
Kids in the park
Are playing "Red Rover."

Lovers are strolling
Down country lanes;
Musicians are playing
Their haunting refrains.

The clock in the steeple
Is chiming the hour;
Sidewalk preachers,
Are extolling God's power.

It's summer again,
And blue sky above;
I wish I was there,
In the hometown I love.

The Circle

The moment we're born,
We start to die;
With every hello,
There must be a good-bye.

The seasons all pass;
The children will grow.
We no sooner arrive,
And it's time to go.

We plant and we harvest;
We sow and we reap.
As soon as we laugh,
It follows we weep.

The pattern of life,
The ebb and the flow,
We try to hold on,
But we have to let go.

As soon as there's darkness,
We look for the light.
We wake in the morning,
To prepare for the night.

The things that we start,
We also must end.
Today you're a stranger,
Tomorrow—my friend!

An Old Fashioned Garden

Come, walk with me in the garden;
Take my hand and stroll by my side.
The sky is blue and the air is clear,
And the path is smooth and wide.

I like to walk in this garden
When the roses are in bloom,
And the lilacs and the daisies
Fill the air with lovely perfume.

There's a spot beneath the willow tree
That's my very own hideaway;
Under its flowing branches
I've spent many a happy day.

There by the sparkling waterfall,
The lilies and violets grow,
And coral bells nod their tiny heads,
When the summer winds gently blow.

Just look at the morning glories,
Growing there by the gate,
And all along the old stone wall,
Hollyhocks stand proudly and straight.

Let's sit for a moment on this little bench,
And tune out the world and its haste;
There is all this beauty surrounding us,
And it's free for our senses to taste.

Oh, look at all the petunias;
Grandmother likes them best.
And sheltered in the apple boughs,
The robins always nest.

There's a spot over in the far corner,
Bright with phlox and columbine;
See how the bees are hovering
On the honeysuckle vine.

The jonquils, tulips and hyacinths
Bloom early in the spring,
And after the long, long winter,
What joy their colors bring!

Over there, where it's always shady,
The ferns grow lush and green.
When the dawn is breaking,
All is peaceful and serene.

Yes, walk with me in the garden
When the shadows of evening are falling.
Together we'll watch as the sun goes down,
And we'll hear the night birds calling.

Then, when the moon is high above,
And the cool night air descends,
We will count the stars as they come out,
And thank God that we are friends.

Autumn in the Black Hills

When it's autumn in the Black Hills,
And the green leaves turn to gold,
Mother Nature takes her palette,
Splashing colors bright and bold.

Yes, it's autumn in the Black Hills,
And it's such a dazzling sight,
Vivid reds and shades of scarlet,
Always changing in the light.

Indian Summer in the Black Hills,
And the days a precious few,
As if time stands still, suspended,
And the world feels fresh and new.

Oh, I know the leaves are turning,
And if I hurry, I'll be there.
Dear Lord, give me one more autumn,
In the pure Dakota air!

Levi Craig Whitcomb

(Born October 25, 1981)

There's a certain little someone,
With eyes of brightest blue,
Who's wrapped himself around my heart,
And I think he knows it, too!

He puts his tiny hand in mine,
And I am filled with joy,
For in that precious baby face,
I see another little boy.

He looks at me with twinkling eyes,
And a tiny turned-up nose.
I love those chubby baby cheeks,
And those dimpled baby toes.

He melts my heart the very way
His daddy used to do,
And I'm at once his willing slave
(His daddy knew that, too).

I never dreamed this grandma role
Would bring me all this bliss.
He twines his arms around my neck
And offers me a kiss.

It seems like only yesterday,
His father was a child.
The memories come flooding back,
How he my heart beguiled.

How wonderful the Master's plan,
This gift that we've been given,
A special way to make our home
A little bit like heaven.

The Land That Time Forgot

In the state of South Dakota,
There's an awesome, mysterious spot,
And God only knows how it came to be,
This land that time forgot.

This place they called the Badlands,
Where the diamondback rattler is king!
And there's naught but the horned toads and lizards,
To herald the coming of spring.

To the west are the beautiful Black Hills,
To the east lie the fertile plains,
Where the cattle are sleek and the corn is green,
Blessed by the soft, gentle rains.

In the blazing sun, the sparse prairie grass
Sprouts in hope, then withers and dies,
And up above in their endless quest,
Are the vultures that circle the skies.

This land is not for the cowards,
Or men who are faint of heart,
For bleached and white are the bones of those
Who came here, but did not depart.

At night when the moon and the stars are bright,
There are phantoms who stalk, so they say,
The ghosts of the timid who wandered in,
And wandering, lost their way.

Water is scarce and hard to find,
And for most it was never found;
The carcasses of man and beast alike,
Lie scattered on the barren ground.

But beauty abounds in this wilderness hell,
And the brave come there to behold
How the peaks transform in the morning sun,
And glow in rich purple and gold.

Yes, only God knows the reason why,
For this wild and desolate spot,
Where the years roll on, but nothing is changed,
In this land that time forgot!

The Sound of Children

There is one very special sound
That's like music to my ear.
It's the sound of children laughing,
When they don't know I'm near.

Their laughter is so genuine,
It fills my heart with joy.
It comes from deep inside of them,
Each little girl and boy.

They laugh at kites a flying,
At butterflies and bees;
They laugh at wind that blows their hair;
They laugh while climbing trees.

When the pace of my life gets too hectic,
All caught up in the noise and the din,
I hear the happy children,
And my world is at peace again.

When all around is confusion,
When only trouble's in sight,
I see the smiling children,
And everything starts to go right.

When I am tired and discouraged,
And things are going all wrong,
Children are like rays of sunshine,
And hope sings a beautiful song.

What would we do without children,
To make living really worthwhile;
They give us purpose and meaning,
With just one lovable smile.

Summer Is Coming!

Those lazy days of summer,
I can tell they are almost here,
When every day is sun-filled,
And skies are blue and clear.

Those easy livin' summer days,
With barefoot children in the parks,
And a myriad tiny fireflies,
Light the night with tiny sparks.

There'll be catfish jumpin' in the ponds;
The meadows will blaze with bloom,
And wafting on the soft warm air,
The wild clover's heady perfume.

Fat dogs will sleep in patches of shade;
Kids will lick dripping ice-cream cones,
And on every bench and porch swing,
You'll see old men warming their bones.

Summer corn will grow tall and green;
There'll be watermelon, juicy and red,
And small boys will be playing tag,
'Til moms call them back home to bed.

And everywhere you look, it seems,
You'll find someone playing softball.
Oh yes, it's almost summertime,
So get ready, one and all!

The Wedding

Upon this lovely April day,
Here in this sacred room,
We've come to share this time of joy,
With our blushing bride and handsome groom.

We wish them roses on life's path,
With just a thorn or two.
We wish them rainbows after rain,
And skies where clouds are few.

May they have happy songs to sing,
Some tears, and more of laughter,
Go boldly now to find their star,
And dreams to follow after.

And as the years pass one by one,
When they are old and gray,
May the love they share be just as sweet,
As it is on this wedding day.

Autumn Romance

There are no seasons of the heart,
And love may lately come.

I was alone and you smiled at me,
You were lonely, too.
The threads of memory that weave the fabric of our lives,
Are only memories, though dear.
You are flesh, alive, and warm.
Your smile brought me happiness;
It felt good to laugh again.

Your hand reached out to me
And I was comforted.
I think that's it—
I feel comfortable in your presence,
As if, somehow, we've known this day would come.

We did not seek each other out,
Was it fate, or circumstance?

It matters not.
I only know that you smiled,
And your smile was welcome.

There are no seasons of the heart,
And love may lately come.

The Dreamer

Some say that I'm an ostrich,
With my head stuck in the sand.
Some say I'm just a dreamer,
That I do not understand.

Some say that I'm a lover,
When there is much to hate.
I like a road that's crooked;
Let others have the straight.

Some call me an optimist,
With a simple point of view.
They say it's rosy glasses
That I am looking through.

Some say that I am foolish,
Wearing blinders on my eyes,
For surely one who thinks as I
Could never be called wise.

Some say that I see only good,
When there's evil all around,
That I hear only harmony,
And not discordant sound.

Some say I live in fairyland,
Where all is fantasy,
With only happy endings,
And not reality.

Of course, I know that this old world
Is not a perfect place;
That doesn't mean that I must go
Through life with frowning face.

I've stubbed my toes and skinned my knees
And wept alone at night,
When things I'd really counted on
Just didn't turn out right.

I've known disappointment;
I've had a broken heart.
When the world I tried so hard to build,
Came falling all apart.

But I believe adversity
Is a blessing in disguise,
And tears are just another way
Of washing out our eyes.

So I don't care what I am called,
It matters not one bit,
For I intend to live my life
The way that I see fit.

I believe if you give your best,
The best will come back to you,
And I believe if you dream enough,
Your dream just might come true!

J Suter

I've Never Seen the Wind

I've never seen the north wind,
But, oh, I know it well.
I've watched the falling snowflakes,
Caught up in winter's spell.

I've never seen the summer wind,
Still, I know its teasing ways,
Stirring in the sultry night,
Sleeping through the lazy days.

I love the winds of springtime,
Blowing softly through the trees,
And although I've never seen it,
I've felt April's gentle breeze.

I've not seen the winds of autumn,
Yet I know that they are there,
Playing havoc 'round the windmills,
Whipping trees 'til they are bare.

I've never been to heaven,
But I know there's such a place.
I've never heard the voice of God,
Or looked upon His face.

Although I've never touched Him,
How good He makes me feel,
And though I've never seen Him,
I know His love for me is real!

Victory

Roses have thorns,
And clouds bring rain.
God has not promised
A life without pain.

But after the rain,
The desert will bloom,
And after death
Is the empty tomb!

God Is Awake!

Have courage, my friend,
God is awake!
He who never sleeps,
Whose eyes go to and fro across the land,
He will hold you
In the hollow of His hand.

Sleep on, dear friend,
And take your rest.
The morning surely comes;
The night was meant for dreamers,
So dream your dreams.
Be unafraid,
All's well, my friend,
God is awake!

Going Back Home to the Farm

(Anderson Farms, Tulare, South Dakota)

There's a place in South Dakota
Where the corn grows tall, and straight,
Where white farmhouses greet the sunlight
And flowers are blooming by the gate.

The cattle graze on endless pasture;
The sheep lie snug within their fold.
Friends are there who make us welcome,
Dearest friends, from days of old.

We talk of times when we were younger—
Those days to us—not long ago,
When our families played together;
Now, we watch grandchildren grow.

The people bred out on this prairie
Are stout of heart, and strong of will,
And we who leave oft feel a hunger
Our busy city life can't fill.

And so, each year we make a journey,
A pilgrimage, back to the farms,
A few short days, but oh, how splendid,
To greet our friends with outstretched arms!

Twilight on the Prairie

When it's twilight on the prairie,
There's a melancholy sky,
As the purple shadows lengthen,
Hear the night birds' mournful cry.

All alone out on the prairie,
Just the tumbleweeds and me,
There's no beginning and no ending,
Like drifting on a grassy sea.

Twilight lingers on the prairie,
As if holding back the night;
The distant sun with waning rays
Reluctantly withdraws its light.

An evening star, then darkness falls,
O'er miles and miles of sod,
All alone out on the prairie,
All alone except for God.

What Have We Done with Christmas?

Come and listen to my story;
It's a tale that must be told.
What have we done with Christmas,
And the Story that's so old?

Long ago in old Judea,
Christ was born to set men free.
Today it seems that Christmas
Is one giant shopping spree!

I think we're starting Christmas
Earlier every year,
So by the time the day arrives,
We're out of Christmas cheer!

Flowers still are blooming,
Grass is growing green,
We start seeing Christmas banners,
Before we've had our Halloween!

We buy for old Aunt Minnie,
Though we really don't know why;
No matter what we give to her,
It just won't satisfy!

And there is cousin Chester,
So stuffy, and a bore,
But still we try to please him;
It's such an awful chore.

It's fun to shop for children,
And then there's dear old gramps.
We should send cards to far-off friends,
But have you seen the price of stamps?

We slave all day at cooking;
Our nerves get worn and frayed.
There are all those great traditions,
And they all must be obeyed.

The banker says we've overdrawn;
Our checkbook is a mess.
There's that "don't leave home without it" card,
You know—the American Express!

Stores make it so appealing;
They don't hasten with your bill.
If VISA doesn't get you,
Master Charge most surely will!

But still, we all love Christmas,
And the joy that Yuletide brings.
It's a time to be a sharing,
Be we commoners or kings.

Christmas is for children;
Christ was once a little child.
We should tell the blessed Story,
Tell of Jesus, meek and mild.

There should be snow at Christmas;
Sleighbells should be ringing.
There should be fires on the hearth,
And choirs should be singing.

There should be time for dreaming,
Quiet moments to be treasured,
And time to count our blessings,
Those things that can't be measured.

We should pray for peace at Christmas,
And the Prince of Peace will hear.
We should read the old, old Story,
And sing carols that are dear.

We should go outside on Christmas Eve,
And search the eastern sky,
To find the Star of Bethlehem;
We can see it if we try.

Let's find the true meaning of Christmas,
And remember God's gift from above.
Let's join hands and hearts together,
And make it a season of love!

December 1982

A Time for Christmas

Christmas is a time for sharing,
A time to show how much we're caring,
A time when we our faith renew,
And pray for peace the whole world through.

Christmas is a time for joy,
Enchanting every girl and boy,
A time to hear the church bells ring,
A time to lift our hearts and sing!

A time to cook and sew and bake,
Cookies, candies, pies and cake,
A time for hearth fires burning bright,
A time for anthems in the night.

A time to put our cares aside,
A time for doors that open wide,
A time to read the Gospel story,
And worship Him, the King of Glory.

A time to be with loved ones dear,
For sending cards that wish good cheer,
A time for trees to decorate,
A time to put aside all hate.

Christmas is that special season,
A time that needs no rhyme or reason,
A time to see the Star above,
But most of all, a time for love!

Of Butterflies and Battlefields

A youth lay dead on the battlefield,
Just as the dawn was breaking,
And far away, in a cottage small,
Was a mother whose heart was aching.

There where the blood was running red,
A flower blossomed so fragile and white;
A butterfly came and hovered above,
As its gossamer wings caught the light.

Now wars are fought, and battles are won,
And the brave are caught up in the fray,
While out in the fields the flowers bloom,
In the dust where the fallen lay.

Beauty mingles with blood on the battleground,
And hope fills the hearts of men;
From the ugly cocoon comes the butterfly,
And man dreams of peace once again.

The butterfly sips the nectar sweet,
Then flies away over the lea;
Mothers still weep, and young men die,
For like butterflies, man must be free!

The Good Shepherd

A Hymn

There's no night that's too black for my Savior.
There's no sorrow that He has not known.
Betrayed by a friend in the garden,
He wept, on His knees, all alone.

There's no sky that's too gray or too cloudy
For the light of His love to shine through,
And the storms that today seem to threaten
Make the skies of tomorrow more blue.

CHORUS:
There's no day that's too long for the Master.
There's no road that's too narrow and steep.
Remember, He's the Good Shepherd,
Longing to comfort His sheep.

There's no fear that He has not conquered.
There are no waves that He cannot calm,
And the bruised and broken body,
He soothes with Gilead's balm.

There's no cross that for Him is too heavy.
There's no task that for Him is too great,
And every prayer He will answer,
If only we patiently wait.

CHORUS:
There's no day that's too long for the Master.
There's no road that's too narrow and steep.
Remember, He's the Good Shepherd.
He lives! and now death is but sleep.

Lord Jesus, Come

A Hymn

Hear our heartfelt supplication.
Oh, God, our Father, hear our call.
Grant us strength for tribulation;
Send Thy blessings to us all.

Thou who art the great Creator,
Our Redeemer and our Friend,
We await Thy Son's returning,
And life with Thee that knows no end.

Though our path be through the valley,
Thou wilt guide our footsteps home;
Though our path be fraught with sorrow,
Even so, Lord Jesus, come!

Come and mend the brokenhearted.
Come and heal the body sore.
Come and fill us with Thy Spirit.
Grant us life forever more.

God's Love

God's love is like a beacon
That shines through every storm;
While the wind and water rages,
He keeps me safe and warm.

God's love is like an anchor,
When the waves are fierce and high;
My ship may toss and tremble,
But I am calm and dry.

God's love is like a healing balm
That soothes when I'm in pain;
He takes my bruised and shattered heart,
And makes it whole again.

God's love is like a banquet,
From His never-ending store,
A wondrous feast, so bountiful,
I will hunger never more.

God's love is a cooling fountain,
In a parched and barren land;
He leads me through the desert waste.
And makes roses bloom in the sand.

God's love is a blessed mystery,
One I can never comprehend,
How He takes such a lowly stranger,
And tells me I am His friend.

The Good Book Says

"Joy cometh in the morning,"
The blessed scriptures say,
And there'll be a bright tomorrow
When the mists have cleared away.

The sun will rise forever;
The skies will all be fair.
There'll be no storms to threaten,
In the homeland over there.

The trump will sound and we'll be changed,
In the twinkling of an eye.
There'll be no pain or suffering,
And no one will have to die.

And in that place called heaven,
The lions won't be wild;
They'll live in perfect harmony,
Led by a little child.

There'll be golden streets and crystal streams,
And mansions bathed in light;
There'll be trees and flowers blooming,
To enthrall us with the sight.

We'll hear the angels singing,
Songs that none have heard before,
And we'll live in peace together,
With our Lord, forever more.

Saints Be Joyful

A Hymn

Look up, look up, oh, saints be joyful;
Wait and watch both day and night.
Soon the heavens will be parted;
Soon we'll see the glorious light.

He is coming. He is coming!
And the clouds will roll away,
Joining voices with the angels,
"Welcome home," we'll hear Him say.

Welcome home, oh, weary pilgrim,
Welcome to the promised land;
Share the joy that now is waiting,
Purchased by His nail-pierced hand.

All the signs down through the ages,
By the prophets prohesied,
Point the way to heaven's portals,
Point to gates that open wide.

There no sin nor death can enter;
There no tears will ever fall.
Look up, look up, oh, saints be joyful.
Christ will come to save us all.

Hallelujah, Advent Day!

A Hymn

We shall stand before the judgment bar,
On that glorious advent day,
When we hear the sound of trumpets,
And the clouds will roll away.

Oh, what joy will fill the faithful,
Those whom Christ has sanctified;
They have kept the ten commandments;
They will be His chosen Bride.

CHORUS:
Hallelujah, hallelujah,
Tis the glorious advent day.
Hallelujah, hallelujah,
All our sins are wiped away.

They are sleeping; they are sleeping,
Waiting for the trumpet call,
All the saints down through the ages;
Soon they'll waken, one and all.

Hear the praises, hear hosanna,
When the graves are opened wide,
When Christ Himself returns to claim them,
With the angels by His side.

CHORUS:
Hallelujah, hallelujah,
Tis the glorious advent day.
Hallelujah, hallelujah,
All our sins are wiped away!

Misery!

What can you do on a winter day,
When the air is cold and the sky is gray,
When the log on the fire is only a glow,
And the rising wind is sure to bring snow?

What can you do when you feel a chill,
And icicles hang from the windowsill,
When your nose is running a steady stream,
And a day in the sun is only a dream?

What can you do when outside it's freezing,
And the sound of your breath is a kind of wheezing?
There's only one thought in your stuffy head,
Turn back the covers and crawl into bed!

Anticipating England

Well, it's off we go to England,
The two of us together.
We plan to have a jolly time,
Regardless of the weather!

We'll smell the roses in the lane;
Big Ben will toll the hour.
We'll watch the changing of the guard,
And gaze on London's Tower.

We'll stroll in Picadilly Square,
And dine at the Savoy.
We may even get to see the Queen—
And won't that bring us joy!

We'll visit Oxford's hallowed halls,
Where learned scholars dwell,
At Stratford-upon-Avon,
We'll fall under Shakespeare's spell.

We'll go to Windsor Castle;
We'll see the Cliffs of Dover,
And as the sea gulls fly on high,
We'll smell the scent of clover.

We'll look down on the river Thames,
And ride an Omnibus.
We'll sip our tea from china cups,
In England, just the two of us!

We'll lift our faces to the sky,
And feel the raindrops fall.
We'll wander through the London fog,
And we won't mind at all!

And when, at last, we bid farewell,
Mem'ries will flood our mind,
Of things we did, and things we saw,
And dear, new friends we'll leave behind.

September 1984

The Randolph Hotel

(Oxford, England, 1984)

Deep in the heart of Oxford,
There's a place that's cast a spell,
Where we were treated just like royalty,
At the famous Randolph Hotel!

The "Spires" cuisine was heavenly,
And there was this to give us joy,
A cozy room, a spot of tea—
And a smile from the concierge, Roy.

Now it's o'er the seas we'll wander,
And it's o'er the world we'll roam,
But when we return to Oxford,
It's the Randolph we'll call home.

So, it's farewell now to England,
But we will return someday,
To the Randolph Hotel in Oxford,
And with concierge Roy we'll stay!

My Flower Bed

I saw a robin with breast so red,
Digging for worms in my flower bed.
''Surely, it must be spring,'' I said.

I watched a rabbit with stealthy tread,
Nibbling tiny green leaves in my flower bed.
I told him ''SHOO!'' and away he fled.

A big fat toad that I nicknamed ''Fred''
Sat blinking his eyes, in my flower bed.
''I think he knows it's spring,'' I said.

There are fluffy white clouds in the sky oe'r head,
And raindrops are falling on my flower bed.
''For certain, it must be spring,'' I said.

A little brown bulb that once looked dead
Is a tuft of bright green in my flower bed.
''Now surely, it must be spring,'' I said.

I saw a pear tree with its branches spread,
To shelter and shade my flower bed.
''I do believe it's spring,'' I said.

The children are playing down by the old shed,
Bright as the buds in my flower bed.
''There's no doubt about it; it's spring,'' I said.

The Quarrel

As gentle as the night falls,
Come on swift feet to my bed,
There's a spot upon the pillow
That's just waiting for your head.

I have counted all the hours,
Passing slowly one by one;
I have searched with eyes gone weary,
And now my wait is done.

I woke at dawn and saw your note,
Like countless times before.
I rushed, too late, to say good-bye;
You had closed the door.

I longed to tell you face to face,
I know now I was wrong.
I had to wait to tell you so,
And oh, the day was long.

Your note just said, "I love you,"
No hint of anger there,
But that was all I needed,
To banish my despair.

I love you, oh, I love you,
And I long to hold you tight.
So come to bed, my darling,
And I'll turn out the light.

I Thank Thee, Lord

For tiny hands that reach for mine,
For trusting eyes so blue,
For little feet that walk with me,
For dimpled cheeks and smiles too,

I thank Thee, Lord.

For steady hands that gently touch,
For arms that hold me tight,
For tender words that speak of love,
For joys he brings from dawn 'til night,

I thank Thee, Lord.

For sturdy walls surrounding me,
For shelter from the cold,
For flowers blooming in the sun,
For friends more dear than any gold,

I thank Thee, Lord.

For every breath that gives me life,
For faith that keeps me strong,
For skies of blue and clouds of white,
For birds that fill the air with song,

I thank Thee, Lord.

For comfort when my heart is sad,
For tears I sometimes shed,
For cleansing when I kneel in prayer,
For hope to face the road ahead,

I thank Thee, Lord.

TELEPHONE
MOUNTAIN BELL

The Telephone's Secrets

If only telephones could speak,
What stories they could tell,
Of heartbreak, and of happiness,
Of heaven, and of hell!

If receivers could paint pictures,
What would the canvas show?
Well-laid plans, or shattered dreams,
In bright colors all aglow.

If the walls of lonely phone booths
Could their secrets with us share,
Real-life dramas, so exciting,
That no soap opera could compare.

But telephones, alas, are silent,
And their walls will mute remain,
Words once spoken, gone forever,
All our wishing is in vain!

Waiting for Spring

A tiny pasqueflower lies fast asleep,
While the snows of winter still cling,
So safe and secure in the rich brown earth,
Just dreaming, and waiting for spring.

Far, far away, in some southern sky,
A meadowlark takes to the wing,
Wending his way to the beautiful hills,
Coming back to welcome the spring.

As the sun warms the sap in the old apple tree,
A bluebell gets ready to ring,
A butterfly stirs in his cozy cocoon,
Each a part of the pageant of spring.

A raindrop that falls from the April sky
Hits the rooftops, making them sing.
In his piney nest, a squirrel hears the sound,
And peeks out to see if it's spring.

A tow-headed boy is down at the pond,
Catching fish with a stick and some string.
A green frog leaps from the mossy bank,
A sign of the coming of spring.

A curly haired girl sits holding her doll,
As she gently rocks in her swing.
And once, long ago, I too was a child,
In the Black Hills, waiting for spring.

The Journey

In faith, one day, I reached for God.
He took me by the hand,
And step by step He led the way,
On the journey He had planned.

I placed myself within His care;
He knows what's best for me.
He goes ahead and clears the path,
Of things I cannot see.

I do not know what lies before;
I trust Him day by day,
And when my eyes are filled with tears,
He wipes them all away.

He leads me on with loving grace,
And though my steps are slow,
He comforts me when I'm in pain,
And shows me where to go.

The road is steep and narrow,
A pathway paved with stone,
But I know that on this journey,
I will never be alone.

My Choice

Dear God, I cannot see tomorrow;
A path of darkness lies ahead.
I do not ask for light to see,
Just strength to follow where I'm led.

The path is rough and I am weak,
And filled with stubborn pride,
Doubting, lest I ought to choose,
A road that's smooth and wide.

Thy feet once trod this narrow way;
Thou knowest every turn.
And, Lord, if Thou my guide will be,
I, too, will strive to learn.

The Legacy

I know these simple words of mine
Will never bring me fame,
And teachers in their ivory towers
Will never speak my name.

The thoughts that flow beneath my pen
Are not profound, or sage;
Instead, a tapestry they weave,
A pattern on each printed page.

That pattern shows my childhood,
Filled with happiness.
I've known a husband's lasting love;
I've shared in his success.

I've raised three lovely children,
Who have filled me with great pride;
I've sweet moments to remember,
By my quiet fireside.

I've looked into my grandson's face;
Like mine, his eyes are blue,
And in his tiny veins there flows
Blood, that's part mine, too.

I've searched my heart and bared my soul,
Within the pages here,
To share my hopes and thoughts and dreams
With those whom I hold dear.

So, precious family and friends,
It's you I'm thinking of,
For even though they're only words,
They are my legacy of love.